ENVISION LEAD GROW

RELEASING THE BOSS WITHIN
WORKBOOK

· · · · ·

Dr Angela D Reddix

· · · · ·

I never expected the success of my book **Envision, Lead, Grow- Releasing the Boss Within**, that it would have received the response that it has. It has been truly a humbling experience. There were a number of requests that I create a workbook to use as a study guide for the book. And so was the genesis of the book you have before you.

In order to get the most out of this workbook, you should read the chapter from Releasing the Boss Within that corresponds with the workbook chapter. Take time and think about each question and exercise. I have left plenty of room for you to write your ideas, and it is my hope that you will refer back to answers as you begin to grow your own business.

For book groups, this workbook contains questions easily adapted for group discussion and opportunities to dive even deeper. If you need copies of this workbook and books for your group, contact us at **Angela@angelareddix.com** to inquire about group sales packages.

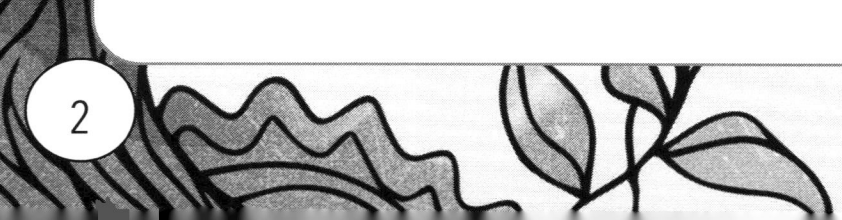

CONTENTS

CHAPTER ONE 4
Little Girls Who Dream

CHAPTER TWO 14
What Makes Your Heart Sing?

CHAPTER THREE 25
Put Pen to Paper

CHAPTER FOUR 36
Speak it and Bring it to Life

CHAPTER FIVE 47
Inhale and Exhale

CHAPTER SIX 58
Delve Into the Details

CHAPTER SEVEN 69
Plan Your Success

CHAPTER EIGHT 78
Reevaluate Your Plan

CHAPTER NINE 89
Stop and Smell the Roses

CHAPTER TEN 96
Congruence

1
CHAPTER ONE

Little Girls Who Dream

In chapter one, I introduced you to scenes from my childhood. Our lives and everything we become start in those formative years.

What were some of your childhood memories, and how did they impact your life?

_____
_____
_____
_____
_____
_____

What things did you believe in your childhood about how your life would turn out that have changed now? Why?

_____
_____
_____
_____
_____
_____
_____

What was your dream job as a child? How close are you to that dream today?

_____
_____
_____
_____
_____
_____
_____

We have different people who impact our lives.
I was influenced by both my mother and grandmother as they were two
powerful women who approached life from different perspectives. I have taken
each of these perspectives into my personality and my beliefs.

Who was influential in your life? Who were your mentors? How did they change your life?

_____
_____
_____
_____
_____
_____
_____
_____
_____
_____

*I discussed my struggles with identity growing up-
and many girls have similar and often even tougher struggles they must face.
I found my tribe in college, and this changed my life and helped me find myself.*

Who is your tribe? How did you find them? How long have they been in your life? How have they changed you?

_____
_____
_____
_____
_____
_____
_____

*Throughout the book I talk a lot about goals and making goals.
I talk about how setting those goals and creating a plan around them is so important if you really want to accomplish them.*

Write about two different goals in your life. One goal you accomplished, and the other you didn't. What were the differences? What strategies to you use to fulfill your goal? What things did you miss with the goal you didn't accomplish?

_____
_____
_____
_____
_____
_____
_____
_____

*One of my favorite stories was about the Tin Woman.
She gave me her wisdom and feedback and I was open to it.
It is not only important to have mentors in our lives,
it is also important to be one for others.*

Who are you a mentor to? Who can you mentor? What wisdom do you think you can share? What do you think others can teach you in return?

_____
_____
_____
_____
_____
_____
_____
_____
_____
_____

*My choice of what to write my dissertation not only changed my life,
but it continues to change lives of young girls around the world.*

What are you doing today to change the world? What can you do tomorrow to change the world even more?

_____
_____
_____
_____
_____
_____
_____
_____

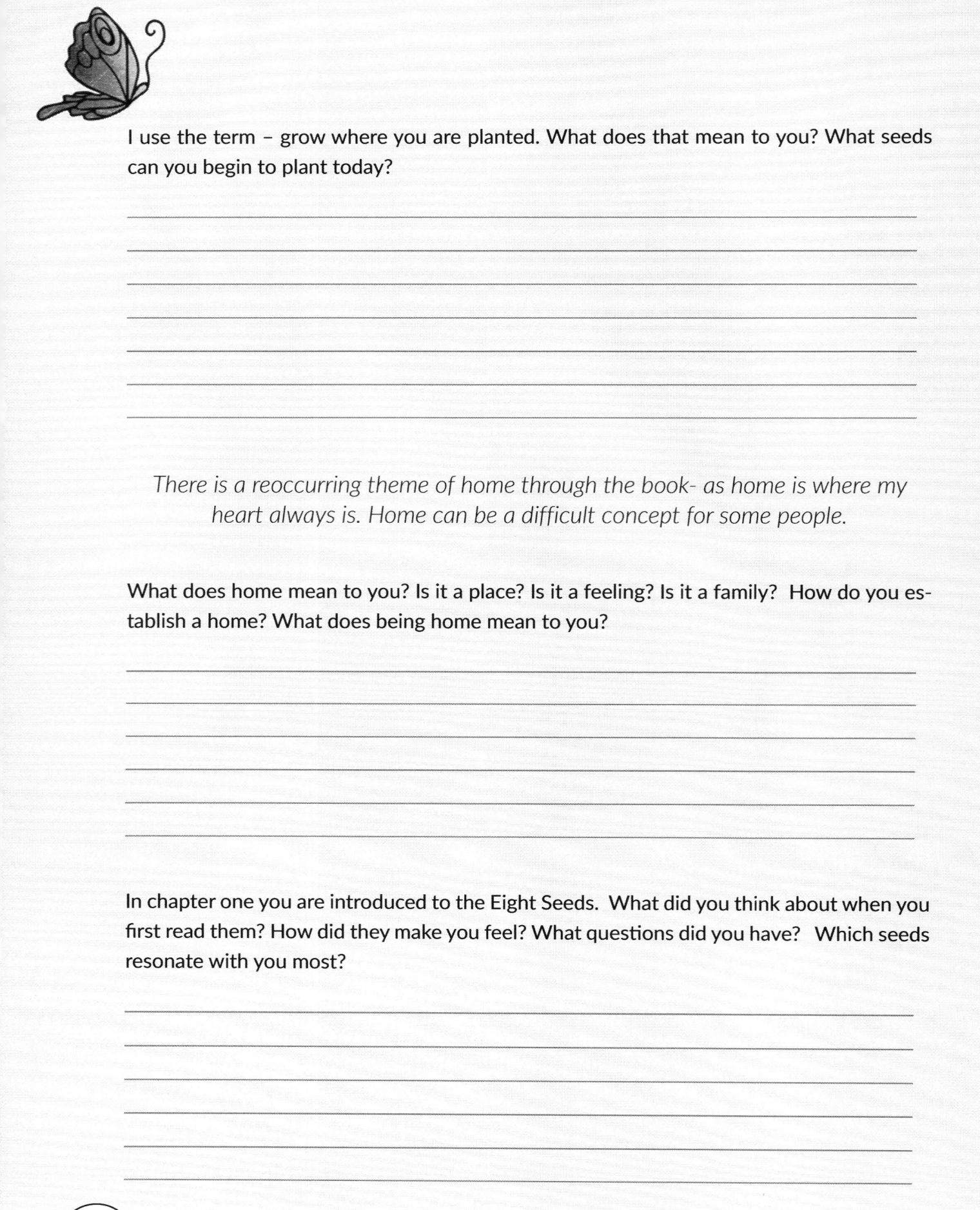

I use the term – grow where you are planted. What does that mean to you? What seeds can you begin to plant today?

_____
_____
_____
_____
_____

There is a reoccurring theme of home through the book- as home is where my heart always is. Home can be a difficult concept for some people.

What does home mean to you? Is it a place? Is it a feeling? Is it a family? How do you establish a home? What does being home mean to you?

_____
_____
_____
_____
_____

In chapter one you are introduced to the Eight Seeds. What did you think about when you first read them? How did they make you feel? What questions did you have? Which seeds resonate with you most?

_____
_____
_____
_____
_____

journal notes

journal notes

journal notes

journal notes

journal notes

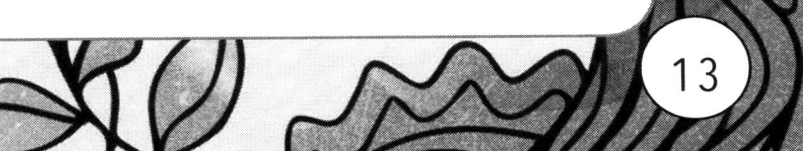

2
CHAPTER TWO

What Makes Your Heart Sing?

*I recount my experience with learning that I had created
a business that was a "two-percenter."
This was a very exciting moment in the evolution of my business.*

What are your huge audacious goals for your business? What will it look like the day you achieve them? What time limits have you created for those goals?

_____
_____
_____
_____
_____
_____
_____
_____
_____
_____
_____
_____
_____
_____
_____

*I remember that moment in Memphis
when I was told nothing good happened there.*

Have there been moments in your life that were so emotional you just knew you were on the right path? What did that feel like? What did you do next?

_____
_____
_____
_____
_____
_____
_____
_____
_____
_____
_____

*Azaria is just one of the amazing girl-bosses
I have had the pleasure of knowing and helping mentor.*

What did you learn from her story? What did you think about Azaria's mother response to Azaria's response to her daughter? Who and what inspires you to want to be more in your life?

_____
_____
_____
_____
_____
_____

TAKE ACTION

*Our desire to explore,
create, sacrifice, and overcome
our obstacles is fueled
by passion.*

*Any endeavor worth pursuing requires passion as its first building block.
We must enter every new venture knowing that it must appeal to
one of our primary passions.*

The discovery of our passion involves identifying the things that make us happiest. When I was a child, I loved dancing and was happiest when I danced—any kind of dancing would do. As I got older, I discovered happiness in so many other things, like traveling and writing. When my career began, I took a deep pleasure in aspects of my work life such as planning, training, and mentoring. Through introspection, I was able to look beyond the surface of what made me happy, discovering what I could do to build my legacy. To pursue our purpose, we must recognize and understand what drives us as individuals.

My mother taught me how to plan for the future. She would sit me down at the dining room table with a chart she had made and ask me, "What do you want to accomplish by the time you are fourteen? Fifteen?" And so on. For each of these ages, she had columns for wealth, family, education, and more. I used this chart to set my goals all the way through my twenties. Back then, I already knew I wanted a doctorate even though I wasn't sure what it was. One of the goals I set for myself every year was that I wanted to make money, my age plus $5,000 (at fourteen that would have been $19,000).

Having something visual and tangible was powerful. At ELG camp, one of the activities I have the girls do is a Passion Board. They are given magazines, scissors, and glue to create a board that represents not only their passion but also a vision of their future.

ACTIVITIES:

1. Identify the activities and dreams that bring you happiness and satisfaction.

2. Be willing to look beyond pursuits that bring you short moments of gratification. Pour your effort into finding the gifts that breathe life into your purpose and add to your legacy.

3. **BUILD YOUR PASSION BOARD** *(instructions below).*
Passion Boards can help you uncover clues you can use to learn about your interests. They help you start to understand what you might want to do as a professional. It isn't only for girls to dream about the future; it's also a lens into our past to remember what our dreams were. A Passion Board can also help you figure out a business idea and build a plan to make it happen. Our passion is made up of the things that make our hearts sing! Once you figure out your passions, you can build a plan that lets you spend as much time with them as possible.

  a. Draw four squares like the one in Figure 1 below. Clear your mind and think big thoughts. In your dreams, what do you want for your future?

  b. In the top left corner of your passion board, write down the things you see for your brightest, most successful future. For instance, you could write, "In my brightest future, I want to own a chain of custom stuffed animal shops, where everyone can build the stuffed animal they've always dreamed of.

  c. In the top right section, write about where you are now. For example, "I own six stuffed animals, but I don't know how they were made. I live near a store that sells custom teddy bears. I've only seen a sewing machine once, and I don't know how to turn it on."

  d. In the bottom left box, write about the tools you'll need to get to the big dream you wrote about in the top left box. "I'll need a sewing machine, lots of different materials like fur & feathers, and buttons, lots of buttons."

  e. In the bottom right box, think about the people you will help, the lives that will change because of your custom stuffed animals. Maybe you'll donate some to the local children's hospital or create an "adopt a stuffed duck" charity to help less fortunate kids.

FIGURE 1

Developing
A Passion Board

What I envision for the future	**Where I Am Right Now**
Tools I Need to Get Where I want to Go	**Who Will I Help Once I Get There**

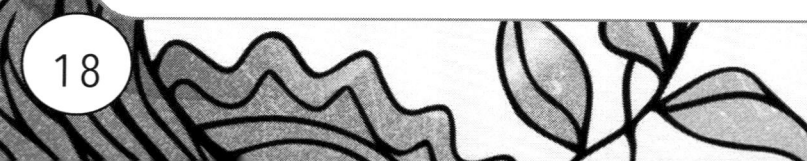

Developing
A Passion Board

Here is the fun part. For each section, find pictures on the web or in magazines that remind you of the things you wrote and add them to each section on the board. Once you've finished, put your Passion Board where you can view it daily. It can be at your desk or next to your bathroom mirror. It can be wherever you can see it and pause to think about your passion and how you can fill your day with it.

journal notes

journal notes

journal notes

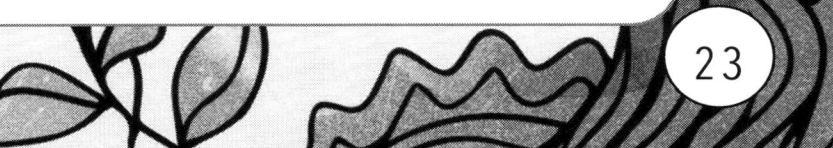

journal notes

journal notes

3
CHAPTER THREE

Put Pen to Paper

I discuss the concept of how experiences create our reality.

How do you feel about this concept? Is it true for you?
How have your experiences changed the course of your life?

_____
_____
_____

Have experiences changed your beliefs? How?

_____
_____
_____

What new experiences are you planning in your life to you achieve your goals?
Create a plan for new experiences and when you'd like to achieve them.

_____
_____
_____
_____
_____
_____

*Writing down your goals
is essential for achieving them.*

How often do you put pen to paper? What is your strategy for writing your eyes down?

_____
_____
_____
_____
_____

How often do your revisit your goals and vision statement? Where do your display your vision statement? How can you get your statement out to more people?

_____
_____
_____
_____
_____
_____

*Once you finish your vision statement,
you need a strategy for achieving that vision.*

Can you use SMART goals for your vision statement? What is the most challenging part of creating SMART?

_____
_____
_____
_____
_____

What are some of the goals you hope to achieve using SMART? What are some of the barriers to your plans?

___

*I shared that I use contracts at home with my husband,
and even though it can be challenging at times,
it does help create accountability in my marriage.*

What are some of the contracts you can create at home? How can you get buy-in to a contract?

___

*A SWOT analysis can be a great way
to assess how your goals are progressing.*

What are some of the challenges you see with SWOT? What are the advantages to using SWOT? How can you structure a regular SWOT analysis in your business?

_____
_____
_____
_____
_____
_____
_____
_____

Nina is another dynamic girl-prenuer.

Where do you see Nina headed in the future? What do you think her challenges will be? What advice would you give her?

_____
_____
_____
_____
_____
_____
_____
_____
_____

ACTIVITIES: TAKE ACTION

We think about all kinds of things throughout the day. If you write down your vision, you are one step closer to success. It doesn't have to be the great American novel. Just write down a few sentences that embody your vision. You can add to it later!

Here are some questions to get you started.

I am at my best when...
___
___
___
___

I am at my worst when...
___
___
___
___
___
___

What do I absolutely love to do?
___
___
___
___
___
___

TAKE ACTION

My natural talents and gifts are:
___
___
___

If I had unlimited time and resources, and I knew I couldn't fail, I would…
___
___
___
___

If I could invite three people to dinner, I would ask…

1. ___
2. ___
3. ___

Now put your answers together.
My vision is:
___
___
___
___
___
___
___
___

journal notes

journal notes

journal notes

journal notes

journal notes

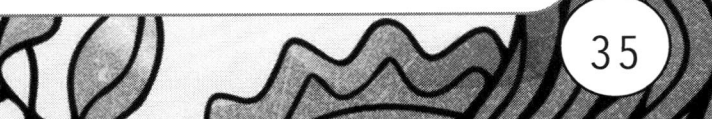

4
CHAPTER FOUR

Speak it and Bring it to Life

*Dr King's speech was very powerful.
Take time to watch him deliver it.*
https://youtu.be/vP4iY1TtS3s

How did that make you feel? What did it make you want to do?

_____
_____
_____
_____

*Take time and watch Robert F Kennedy
as he announces the death of Martin Luther King.*
https://youtu.be/GoKzCff8Zbs

How do you feel after that speech? What do the words move those listening to do? What does he do in order to inspire those listening?

_____
_____
_____
_____

How can you use your words to inspire those around you? How can you inspire others to join you in your vision?

___

*Developing an elevator pitch can be powerful
- not only to be prepared but to also hone your message.*

What would you include in your elevator pitch? Who would you most like to deliver it to? How can you make your dream pitch a reality?

___

Chanel has been a blessing to me and our company.

What did you notice about Chanel's story? What did you learn from her story? What resonated most in your life and story?

ACTIVITIES: TAKE ACTION

Speak it and Bring it to Life

Imagine you are on the dream trip of a lifetime: a safari in Africa. Would you leave unprepared? Or would you plan that trip?

You would pack the right clothes, bug spray and sunscreen, and of course, have a camera ready to take pictures. You would hold that camera in your lap the whole time, prepared to catch anything of value you saw on that journey.

It could take months of preparation!

Preparing an elevator speech takes planning as well. It should be concise, to the point, and you must be ready to share it on a moment's notice. Getting it right takes time and a little practice, but when the time comes, you will be prepared.

How can you capture someone's attention is just one minute? Imagine it is a person who can make your dreams come true—someone like Oprah. Below is a simple template you can follow. Spend time working on the answers and write them down. Put your pitch on an index card and practice it in front of a mirror. Then try it out with your friends and family.

You've got this!

Activities:
Take Action

Define Who You Are:
Write one sentence about who you are.

Describe What You Do:
Using your mission statement as a guide, write one to two sentences about what your skills and accomplishments are.

State Your Goal:
Identify and define what you're passionate about and what you're striving toward in life.

Give your "Why":
State what makes you unique and why your audience should invest their interest in you.

Activities:
Take Action

ACTIVITIES:

1. Define Who You Are: Write one sentence about who you are.

_____
_____
_____
_____

2. Describe What You Do: Using your mission statement as a guide, write one to two sentences about what your skills and accomplishments are.

_____
_____
_____
_____

3. State Your Goal: Identify and define what you're passionate about and what you're striving toward in life.

_____
_____
_____

4. Give your "Why": State what makes you unique and why your audience should invest their interest in you.

_____
_____
_____
_____

journal notes

journal notes

journal notes

journal notes _____

journal notes

5
CHAPTER FIVE

Inhale and Exhale

*Inhaling and exhaling are the essential components of life.
Yet, sometimes we forget to just breathe.*

What does inhaling and exhaling look like in your life? In your business? In your relationships?

_____
_____
_____
_____
_____

*I talk about my Pink Cadillac journey.
Even though that was a number of years ago,
I still use many of the strategies I learned back then.*

Do you have a pink Cadillac story? Who are your influencers? What would it be like to meet one of them in person?

_____
_____
_____
_____
_____

*I believe we all have Dorothy moments from time to time in our lives-
that moment when we realize we had the answers we were seeking all along.*

What has been your Dorothy moment? What answers did you find you already knew?

_____
_____
_____
_____
_____

What strategies do you use from other careers? How do they translate from business to another?

_____
_____
_____
_____
_____
_____

*I have been blessed to have a wonderful collection of people
around me that have helped me breathe life into my vision.*

What did you think about Monica's story? What did you learn? How can you apply what you have learned to your own company?

_____
_____
_____
_____
_____
_____

*Letting people go from our lives
can be very hard and emotional.*

What people have you let go recently? Why?

_____
_____
_____
_____
_____

What people do you need to let go? What is holding you back?

_____
_____
_____
_____
_____
_____
_____

What strategies do you use to let people go? How effective are they?

_____
_____
_____
_____
_____
_____
_____

RELATIONSHIPS

The leaves are people who are only there for a season and are won't be around long-term.

The buds are people you are developing relationships with, that you think could be meaningful once more effort is put into the relationship.

The branches are the people who have been around for some time and will probably stay, but if there is too much adversity, they won't stick around.

The trunk of the tree represents those who have been your support system.

The roots are the people who hold you down no matter what tornadoes, hurricanes, or rain life throws your way.

RELATIONSHIPS
Who are the people that represent your:

- leaves
- buds
- branches
- trunk
- roots

ACTIVITIES: TAKE ACTION

Relationships are a lot like a tree. They need love, care, and nurturing like a tree, and not all parts are created equal. Think about the people in your life and what part of the tree they are:

THE LEAVES are people who are only there for a season and won't be around long term.

THE LEAVES _____

THE BUDS are people you are developing relationships with, whom you think could be meaningful once more effort is put into the relationship.

THE BUDS _____

THE BRANCHES are the people who have been around for some time and will probably stay, but if there is too much adversity, they won't stick around.

THE BRANCHES _____

THE TRUNK of the tree represents those who have been your support system.

THE TRUNK _____

THE ROOTS are the people who hold you down no matter what tornadoes, hurricanes, or rain life throws your way.

THE ROOTS _____

journal notes

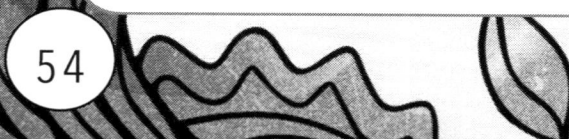

journal notes

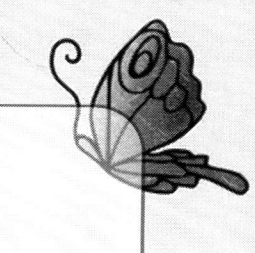

journal notes

journal notes

journal notes

6
CHAPTER SIX

Delve Into the Details

In advertising, there is a lot of "overnight success" stories in order to sell a product or service.

What is your response when you see or hear these types of stories? Why do you think these stories are used, and are they successful?

_____
_____
_____
_____
_____
_____

I discuss the three types of knowledge.

What things do you know that are helping you in your business today?

_____
_____
_____
_____
_____
_____
_____
_____

What things do you know that you DON'T know in your business today? What is your plan for dealing with those things?

_____
_____
_____
_____
_____
_____

What things have been a surprise in your business? What was the outcome of those surprises? What can you do in the future to lessen and negative effects to your business?

_____
_____
_____
_____
_____
_____
_____

Partnerships do matter.
It is really hard to create something big- alone.

Who have you developed strategic partnerships with? Who would you like to partner with?

_____
_____
_____
_____
_____

What challenges have you faced when creating partnerships? What fears do you have in partnerships?

_____
_____
_____
_____
_____

I had to pivot quickly early on in the formation of ELG.

How do you deal with pivots in your business? What can you do to prepare for the unknowable? Who can you count on?

_____
_____
_____
_____
_____

In Danielle's story she paid attention to the details and it paid off for her?

What did you learn from her story? What can you use from her story in your own business?

_____
_____
_____
_____
_____

How is your idea different?	**How will you market your ideas?**
Is there funding available?	**What do you need to have in place to move forward?**

Finding the answers to the big and small questions will ensure your success. The better information you have, the more accurate your planning can be. This means research, and for some people, research can sound intimidating.

ACTIVITIES: TAKE ACTION

*Dreaming is fun, but you also have to dig in and
figure out how to effectively do what you envision.*

Take time to research individuals or companies doing similar things to those you are interested in and figure out how to fit into the marketplace.

How is your idea different?

_____
_____
_____
_____

How will you market your ideas?

_____
_____
_____
_____

Is there funding available?

_____
_____
_____
_____

What do you need to have in place to move forward?

_____
_____
_____
_____

Finding the answers to the big and small questions will ensure your success. The better information you have, the more accurate your planning can be. This means research, and for some people, research can sound intimidating.

Fill out the form below to begin to learn how to research companies. Have fun with it!

journal notes

journal notes

journal notes

journal notes

journal notes

7
CHAPTER SEVEN

Plan Your Success

*If you want to have success in your business
- you have to prepare for it.*

What is your success plan? Who is involved in your success plan?
___
___
___
___

*Project management is an essential component of a business,
especially when your business has growing pains.*

How do you handle project management?
___
___
___
___

What have your successes been in project management? What have you failures looked like? What can you do better in the future?
___
___
___
___

How do you assess a projects process? Do you have a formal strategy in place? What does your strategy look like?

_____
_____
_____

There is no such thing as a business without risk.

How do you assess risk in your business? How do you mitigate risk?

_____
_____
_____

What strategies do you have in place that can mitigate risk on an ongoing basis?

_____
_____
_____

Mentors like Pam have been essential in ELG.

What did you learn from Pam's story? How can you take what you have learned and apply it to your business?

_____
_____
_____

How does planning help your business? How often do you plan and reassess?

_____
_____
_____

ACTIVITY: TAKE ACTION

Between now and the end of the year, set some goals for yourself to get to where you want to be.

GOALS

Between now and the end of the year, you want to set some goals for yourself to get to where you want to be. Try to come up with a list of twenty goals that you can achieve in the next twelve months.

These will serve as milestones for you to ensure you are on track to reaching your ultimate goals.

For example, if you are starting a baking company, a goal you set for yourself in the next month is to try three new recipes for desserts and see which ones are the best. Then, in the following month, you want to try three different recipes. You can set goals for your business as well as personal goals, like improving your health.

20 GOALS 12 MONTHS

GOALS

1. _____
2. _____
3. _____
4. _____
5. _____
6. _____
7. _____
8. _____
9. _____
10. _____
11. _____
12. _____
13. _____
14. _____
15. _____
16. _____
17. _____
18. _____
19. _____
20. _____

journal notes

journal notes

journal notes

journal notes

journal notes

8
CHAPTER EIGHT

Reevaluate Your Plan

*Plans that are static, tend to be like cornstalks during a tornado
- if they cannot bend, they break.
Reevaluating your plan is essential for growth.*

What did you learn about the Netflix story? How does it apply to your business or industry? Do you feel you are prepared to pivot?

_____
_____
_____
_____
_____

*Being a leader of a company means making decisions,
and then acting upon those decisions.*

Have you found it hard to make decisions in your business and sticking to them?

_____
_____
_____
_____
_____

What process do you have for making important business decisions?
Who do you involve?

_____
_____
_____
_____
_____

How do you role out new policies and directions for your company?
How do you get buy in?

_____
_____
_____
_____
_____
_____

Many companies either do not grow because of analysis paralysis
- leaders look for perfection and the removal of risk.

How has analysis paralysis played out in your business? How do you deal with it?

_____
_____
_____
_____
_____

Do you believe in the idea that being done is better than perfect?
What metrics do you use to move a project along to completion?

___

How do you deal with reporting in your company?
How often do you touch base with others in leadership roles?

___

*Anyssa had a dream, and took a stand.
Even though she changed direction later, she held her stand.*

What is your stand? What hill are you "willing to die on" (meaning what situations will you not budge based on your values and beliefs)?

___

Using the tool below, take a moment and draw a picture of how you would describe how you plan to end this week.

ACTIVITY: TAKE ACTION

Learning to pivot is essential to growth. Let's see how well you pivot throughout a week.

By the end of the week, I plan to have finished xyz.

_____
_____
_____
_____
_____
_____

Throughout the day, there are detours and barriers to reaching the planned destination (the picture we drew). Document your daily journey and identify the roadblocks that you encountered.

DETOURS _____   ROADBLOCK _____

DETOURS _____   ROADBLOCK _____
_____   _____
_____   _____
_____   _____
_____   _____
_____   _____
_____   _____

DETOURS _____   ROADBLOCK _____
_____   _____
_____   _____
_____   _____
_____   _____
_____   _____
_____   _____

DETOURS _____   ROADBLOCK _____
_____   _____
_____   _____
_____   _____
_____   _____
_____   _____
_____   _____

How many times did you create a solution to an unplanned obstacle?

_____
_____
_____
_____
_____
_____

Did you reach your final destination? If not, why not?

_____
_____
_____
_____
_____
_____
_____

And what were your lessons learned?

_____
_____
_____
_____
_____
_____
_____
_____

journal notes

journal notes

journal notes

journal notes

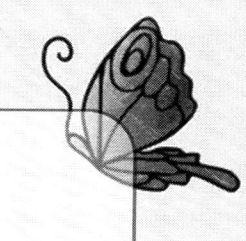

journal notes

CHAPTER NINE

Stop and Smell the Roses

Many of us are brought up believing that we must work hard to succeed, but the message of when to rest is often missing.

What do you do to unwind? Do you build in time to smell the roses?

_____
_____
_____
_____
_____

Do you give those you work with time to breathe and replenish? How important is this?

_____
_____
_____
_____

What kind of culture have you cultivated in your business? Does it include fun?

_____
_____
_____
_____
_____

*Milestones are important ways to take
a breath and celebrate how far you have come.*

What milestones have you set for your business? What kinds of celebrations surround those milestones?

_____
_____
_____
_____

It can be tough to take leaps of faith as demonstrated in Aralyn's and Heidi's story.

What things stood out in their story? How can use what you have learned into your own life?

_____
_____
_____
_____
_____
_____
_____

What is the "why" in your business? How do you include that "why" in every aspect of your business?

_____
_____
_____
_____
_____

ACTIVITIES: TAKE ACTION

Take time each day, or at least each week, to really appreciate what you've built.

We are often so busy and lost in the details of our work that we don't truly value what we've done. You may have hundreds of employees, but how do you make their lives better?

You may be solving critical issues for your clients, but how are you making an impact?

You may be providing a resource that saves a life. How does that feel? Enjoy what you've cultivated…you deserve it!

*Reflection*_____
_____
_____
_____
_____
_____
_____
_____
_____
_____
_____
_____
_____
_____
_____
_____
_____

journal notes

journal notes

journal notes

journal notes

10
CHAPTER TEN

Congruence

Congruence is so important as it pulls everything together in your business and life.

What congruence do you see in your business and life?

_____
_____
_____
_____
_____

How can you bake congruence into your business as it grows?

_____
_____
_____
_____
_____

Planning for the next thing can help you grow your current business faster as you set a new goal for the future.

What is the next act in your business? What is its connection to your current business?

_____
_____
_____
_____

What plans are you developing to grow a new business? Do you have a formal plan or is it just and idea?

_____
_____
_____
_____

What do you need to grow a new seed? Who are your new partners? What do you need financially to grow that new business?

_____
_____
_____
_____
_____

In the end I define what Envision, Lead, Grow means to me.

What does Envision mean to your business?

_____
_____
_____
_____

_____
_____
_____
_____

What does leading look like in your business now you have read the book and worked your way through this workbook?

_____
_____
_____
_____
_____

What does growing your business look like now? What are your next steps you can begin after putting this workbook down?

_____
_____
_____
_____
_____

Legacy is an investment in the lives of those who will come after us.

What legacy would you like to leave? How do you plan to create that legacy?

_____
_____
_____
_____
_____

ACTIVITY: TAKE ACTION

In my talks, I often ask the participants to write a letter to themselves as a self-commitment. I collect their notes, and in six months, the messages they wrote are mailed back to them. They can see what they promised themselves and determine how well they are doing.

What is the promise you will make to yourself?

When you are done, seal the envelope and write on it "Open on…"
Write a date six months in the future.

_____
_____
_____
_____
_____
_____
_____
_____

*"You have plenty of courage, I'm sure,"
answered Oz.*

"All you need is confidence in yourself."

There is no living thing that isn't afraid when it faces danger. The true courage is in facing danger when you are afraid, and that kind of courage you have in plenty."

— L. Frank Baum, The Wonderful Wizard of Oz

journal notes

journal notes

journal notes

journal notes

journal notes

journal notes

journal notes